How to Write a Killer Sales Résumé

COPYRIGHT INFORMATION

DISCLAIMER

CONTENTS

FOREWORD

Q. What is the single most important question that your sales résumé must answer for any employer?

A. "How can this person help grow my business?"

After your sales résumé hits the recruiting manager's desk, your résumé has 'at best' 10 seconds to impress them that you are worthy of further consideration.

10 seconds, that's all!

Why? Because recruitment managers are busy and they are inundated with applicants to choose from. When they look at the pile of sales résumés that land on their in-tray or email Inbox, you can be sure that they are going to be ruthless in cutting through all of the time-wasters and tire-kickers.

Your résumé has got to stand out from the rest of the pile.

Good sales jobs are highly sought after. Attractive pay, good perks, and a reasonable degree of freedom are but a few of the factors that make sales jobs so desirable. And the competition is fierce, both from people fresh out of college as well as experienced sales professionals looking to step up their pay grade. Good jobs are hard to come by!

This book shows you how to create a targeted, dazzling résumé that will present your skills and experience in a positive and accurate light matching the requirements of the position that you are applying for as closely as possible.

Matching your résumé precisely to the needs of the position increases your chance of securing an interview.

The skills you are about to learn equip you with the expertise you need to create a winning résumé so that if and when you need to change jobs then you'll be able to initiate that change – without any fancy 3rd party software or needing to outsource the task to an expensive résumé service.

You'll be independent from the crowd in more way than one!

Sincerely,

C. Beaumont

February 17th.

How to Write a Killer Sales Résumé

INTRODUCTION – YOU'RE IN SALES - SELL YOURSELF!

OK – SO WHO IS GOING TO BUY ME?

A sales person's most important product is themself.

So, it stands to reason that *being in sales,* sales people spend time and effort selling themselves – especially when applying for jobs.

Of course, this sales pitch must embrace dress, speech, attitude, behavior and manner plus a whole lot more besides. But when it comes to applying for jobs - through the job application and résumé path - then the first point of contact with the recruiters or hiring manager, is not you but **your résumé!**

To a certain extent, this point is the same for all disciplines, but it is especially relevant for sales people.

You may be brilliant and perfect for the job, *but* if your résumé does not get noticed and does not convey the appropriate qualities, then you *are* going to get passed over. A well-crafted sales résumé really puts you head and shoulders above the crowd.

The information that follows will show you how to capture your skills, accomplishments, experience, and education in a targeted, eye-catching, and exciting manner in such a way that you will be noticed and **more importantly - you will be granted interviews**!

GETTING A JOB – JUST WHERE DOES THE RÉSUMÉ FIT IN?

Getting a job is generally a three-step process. First, you identify the job that you want. Second, you apply for the job by supplying the prospective employer with your résumé and cover letter. Then finally, you attend an interview to secure the job.

Of course, you already have the first step covered: you know that you want a sales job in your particular field.

This book addresses the next step - the preparation of razor sharp, killer résumés (and cover letters) **that will get you job interviews**.

Note: an important qualifier – the role of the résumé is not to get you a job – the résumé's function is to get you an **interview**. The function of the interview is to get you the job.

The interview stage – how to prepare and act during the interview – is really another book in its own right and is not dealt with here. For more information on this subject, refer to the resources section of the book or visit www.WriteASalesResume.com for some useful recommendations.

Regardless of your circumstances, once you have read this book then you'll know how to optimize your skills, background, qualifications, and interests to prepare a winning sales résumé.

HOW TO USE THIS BOOK

My recommendation is for you to read the book from beginning to end first - without actually starting work on your résumé. This will give you a feel for what is required as well as presenting the overall process (don't worry, it's simple!).

Then work through the book while actually writing your sales résumé, heading directly to the appropriate chapter that matches your level of sales experience.

As you work through this book, you'll come across various examples that are there to demonstrate a point. The examples will be pitched to a particular role in a certain industry. Naturally, these examples may not necessarily be from your industry. That doesn't matter - the point is to understand the message being conveyed so that you can then apply this information to your own sales résumé.

Ready? Ok, let's get started...

1

SELL YOURSELF WITH YOUR RÉSUMÉ

THE ELEMENTS OF A WINNING SALES RÉSUMÉ

1. CHRONOLOGICAL RÉSUMÉ FORMAT

There are many format styles for résumés. However, the best one for a sales résumé, regardless of the level of experience is – a chronological format. A chronological résumé is simply a logical way to present your various skills, achievements, work experience, and qualifications. In particular, it presents your work experience in a chronological order, starting with your current job and then working back in time.

The other résumé formats - not discussed here - are the functional résumé (a skills orientated résumé, for people who have skills & experience, but not a regular track history of work – for instance someone returning to work after a break) and the combination résumé format, which is best suited to consultants or those with a combination of skills of experience and varied work history.

2. THE BASIC RÉSUMÉ WRITING PRINCIPLES

When writing résumés in general, it's important to write your résumé in a concise, accurate, descriptive, rounded, and exciting way. The prose may not always be grammatically correct, but the style described is the best way to write a good résumé. It is the most effective technique to highlight your capabilities. This is discussed in chapter 2 - Résumé Writing Basics, where you'll learn the '17 winning principles that'll sell your résumé.'

3. RÉSUMÉ STYLE – IT DEPENDS ON EXPERIENCE

Given your degree of experience and the seniority of the position that you are applying for, your résumé will have a slightly different form. These two main forms are discussed in separate chapters.

    a) Chapter 3 - Entry Level & Non Executive Positions

    b) Chapter 4 - Experienced Personnel & Executive

In each chapter you will learn about the style and the content that should be included in that style of sales résumé.

4. TARGET YOUR SALES RÉSUMÉ

As you work through this book and you actually write your résumé, it's quite possible that you'll be preparing for a particular job (like an ad that you saw advertised or heard about) or you may simply be getting your résumé in shape for a job search coming up in the future.

Either way, understand that you will probably need to 'customize' your résumé for each job that you apply for.

In my experience, this is where most sales résumés fail!

Your new résumé could be written for a general sales job or it may be perfect for posting to job websites or sending out on a speculative basis to recruitment agencies and head-hunters. But when you are applying for a **particular position** you'll need to tweak the contents of your sales résumé so that it fits the job description of the role. Let me explain...

Here's where 90% sales résumés fall down

Many people fail to focus on the **specific** requirements of the job that they are applying for. They often have a single résumé that they use for *all positions*, for *all* job applications and sometimes (even worse) for *all* industries.

They have one **catch-all** sales résumé that is sent out in the hope that it catches whatever sales job they happen to be applying for. This one-size-fits-all résumé strategy is very common - and it's highly ineffective.

So, with this book, you'll learn how to take your résumé (either based on chapter 3 or chapter 4) and then use a few simple techniques to target it to the job that you are applying for. This targeting technique is discussed in chapter 5.

The targeted approach is a bit more work as each new position will need a tailored sales résumé but on the up-side, your rate of obtaining interviews will shoot up! Overall, this is a winning approach.

5. THE RÉSUMÉ COVER LETTER

When it comes to the actual job application, then you'll need a good cover letter to accompany your sales résumé. Every job application should be accompanied by a clear concise cover letter.

Your cover letter will be brief - just a couple of paragraphs long - and will make sure that the employer **wants to read your résumé.** Skip cover letters at your peril - good cover letters are important!

They are discussed in chapter 6.

6. RESOURCES

To help make your résumé writing task a bit easier, I have included a few resources in the appendix, such as:

Key Action Words

You must populate your résumé with strong descriptive action words that demonstrate your achievements, capabilities, and strengths. There are over 300 action words to get you started.

Résumé Templates

Want to see at a glance just what makes up a sales résumé? If so, then look at the two sales résumé templates. They contain the basic ingredients that make up both an entry level / non-executive sales résumé and an experienced personnel / executive sales résumé

Résumé Examples

Examples of both an entry level / non-executive sales résumé and an experienced personnel / executive sales résumé are provided to show how these look.

Additional Resources

Just in case, you need them or your résumé writing and job hunting, the following additional resources are included like:

- Job websites

- Industry specific guidance

- Interview help

I should hope that after reading this book you wouldn't need either of these products, but just in case...

- Résumé writing services

- Résumé writing software

IN SUMMARY

Here are the highlights of what has been discussed:

1. Use a chronological résumé format

2. Follow basic résumé writing principles

3. Choose the correct résumé style as per your level of professional experience

4. Take the time to target your résumé to fit the job position

5. Write an excellent résumé cover letter to go with the résumé

6. Check out the additional resources if you need help

2

WRITING

RÉSUMÉ BASICS

17 WINNING PRINCIPLES THAT WILL SELL YOUR RÉSUMÉ

What we're going to look at here are the essential principles for writing winning résumés. This is a series of résumé writing basics, which are fundamental to the creation of a great résumé.

Integrate these same elements into your sales résumé for a head start on the rest of the competition.

Two main questions you need to consider before we get started are -

1. Who is going to read your résumé?

2. Who should you write your résumé for?

Your résumé could be read by a multitude of different parties including:

- Independent agency recruiters

- Computer scanning software (which we look at in some detail later)

- Corporate recruitment staff who may be screening applicants and

- Recruiting managers - the decision makers - who decide which applicants to interview and which to hire

Your résumé must appeal to all of these interested parties. Bearing this in mind, let's get started…

1. YOUR RÉSUMÉ SHOULD BE TWO PAGES OR LESS – NOT MORE …

Your résumé should be no longer than two pages - if it is, then you need edit it down. A single page résumé is fine. Remember you want to impress the employer, not bore them.

Make it easy for the employer to see that you are the ideal candidate. You don't want them to have to wade through pages of data to search for the relevant data. If you do, then you risk the chance that the employer will miss something important.

2. MAKE YOUR RÉSUMÉ BRIEF, ACCURATE, EASY TO READ AND PLEASANT TO THE EYE...

Look at it this way: if the employer has to read 150 résumés, then you must make it easy for the employer to spot YOU over the other 149 applicants.

3. MAKE THE MOST OF PAGE 1...

The most important information needs to be on page 1 of your résumé. This is where you will highlight your best and most relevant skills and experience.

If you have work experience in…

1. Marketing experience

2. Project management experience

3. Sales experience

4. You worked as a janitor for 6 months when you first left high school

...then the order of importance for a sales résumé is going to be

1. Sales

2. Marketing

3. Project management

Drop the janitor job from your résumé, unless you really feel it supports your application in some way.

4. STATE YOUR ACHIEVEMENTS...DO NOT BE MODEST!

This is a competition - you must really sell yourself. Your achievements should relate to factors that are relevant to your application and that will impress the recruiter. By way of example, these achievements can include:

*   Sales achievements

*   The number of times you beat your quota

*   Awards received

*   Campaigns you ran

*   Customers you acquired

*   Business you grew

*   Areas (product or geographical) you moved into

*   Costs you saved

*   Strategic measures you initiated

*   Joint ventures you ran

*   Business development measures

*   Leads you generated

Don't forget to emphasize other skills such as:

- Negotiating skills

- Communication skills

- Presentation skills

5. WRITE IN THE FIRST PERSON...

This means writing from your point of view as though you are saying – 'I did this.' However, you don't want to use the word 'I' very much at all. You need to convey this word without actually using it. Here are several examples.

- I achieved 150% growth in my personal sales over 12 months. This sentence simply becomes...

  ◊ **Achieved 150% growth in sales over 12 months**

- I was responsible for recruiting an additional 35 people to meet increased product demand. This now becomes...

  ◊ **Recruited extra 35 people to meet increased product demand.**

Do you see that by removing the word 'I' subtly creates a sharper, higher impact sales résumé?

6. USE VERBS – ACTION WORDS...

Use action verbs such as **achieved, accomplished, delivered, grew, managed, engineered, and facilitated** as much as is possible.

Try to start each sentence with an action word. Action words get you noticed since they demonstrate 'the value that you can contribute to the new company.' They show that you can deliver the goods. Remember the employer is always asking, "What can this person do for my business?"

If you are stuck for suitable action words then look at the appendix section - Key Action Words List for a list of great power words that you can weave into your résumé.

7. REMOVE ARTICLE WORDS WHERE POSSIBLE...

Do not pad your résumé with useless words.

- Aim to write your résumé punchy and to the point

- As previously pointed out, start by removing the word '**I**'

- Additionally, you should **minimize the use of article words** such as **the, a,** and **an**

By removing these simple words, you will make your résumé tighter, better focused and a more enjoyable read.

Compare these two sentences:

I managed a team of 10 sales representatives over a period of three years during which time we were able to grow the sales turnover by 400%.

Managed team of 10 sales representatives and grew sales by 400% in three years.

8. SIZE AND DETAILS COUNT...

Add numbers to convey **size** and **growth**.

Example 1:

Poor statement:

I managed a sales team

Better statement:

Managed team of 30 sales people

The bottom version is stronger, has greater resonance without the two extra words, and by adding the **size** of the sales team you have added weight / dimension to an otherwise vague statement. It's important to be as detailed and as accurate as possible.

Example 2:

Poor statement:

I grew my personal sales in twelve months

Better statement:

Achieved 150% sales growth in 12 months

In the improved statement, **I** and **my** were removed and the action verb **achieved** was added. This new statement has a tangible level of growth (150%).

Another sample statement:

Grew sales from $900k to $1,350k in 12 months

This statement is also very good and in some ways better since it conveys size as well as growth. If the details are impressive then state them. Otherwise, don't worry.

9. USE OF NUMBERS...

The convention of spelling out numbers 'one - nine' and using digits for 'ten and above' is fine, **except when referring to large sums of money**.

$3 million reads better than **three million dollars**

10. BE POSITIVE ...

Avoid negativity - only present information in a positive way. Negativity and sniping looks bad so don't do it! If something can only be perceived negatively, **then do not mention it**.

11. STATE GOOD POINTS AND OMIT BAD POINTS...

This may be stating the obvious, but only make statements or state facts about matters you are happy to talk about and expand upon in an interview. If that's not the case with some particular issue, then do not put them in your résumé.

12. BORROW CREDIBILITY

If you have had the good fortune (or the acumen) to work with/for a sizeable company that is –

1. Fortune 1000 company and / or

2. Has a great $ annual turnover and / or

3. Is industry respected for some reason

-then you can add impact and credibility to your résumé by borrowing that company's inherent credibility. You can name drop / quote it's annual turnover (assuming that that information was not confidential of course) and mention anything else it is impressive.

Information that is worth mentioning includes:

• It's a $50B turnover company

• It has 10,000 employees worldwide

• It developed a cure for the common cold

13. SHOULD YOU TELL THE TRUTH?

This should be obvious. **Do not lie on your résumé**. Aside from the ethical issues, you might get caught in an interview that will get you sidelined immediately.

Experienced interviewers are well-versed in spotting non-truths - so don't tempt fate.

14. SPELLING

You can take liberties with your grammar as per the above techniques, but ensure that there are no spelling mistakes. The easiest way to do this, once you have completed writing your résumé, is to spell check it.

Still it is easy for errors to remain. At this point, print it off, read it over aloud for errors, and then have a friend check it over. In this way, you will make sure you are sending out a perfectly clean copy of your résumé.

15. INFORMATION TO OMIT FROM YOUR RÉSUMÉ

You want to be assessed for a job position based upon your skills and experience that you bring to a role. Therefore, you should not mention anything in your résumé that doesn't directly support your professional objectives.

So, unless any of the following directly support your application, omit them from your résumé:

- Racial origin

- Sexual orientation

- Height

- Weight

- Religion

- Hobbies

- Race

- Disabilities

- Age

- Place of birth

- Picture – only include if it is required

As I said before – don't mention anything that you don't want to talk about in the interview. If it's on your résumé, the interviewer is free to ask about it. Beware!

Omitting all of this *off-target* information from your résumé keeps it clutter free, allowing the interviewer to focus on the important material. It also removes the element of bias, which (perhaps) could otherwise creep in.

16. PROBLEM-ACTION-RESULT (PAR)

When presenting your career experience, if a course of action was a solution to a problem, and then try to convey what the **problem** was, the **action** you took and the subsequent **result** - PAR.

For example...

Closed down three loss-making accounts - which saved $300k per annum.

Another example...

By changing product set, turned around three loss-making accounts in 6 months – turned from losing $50k per month to earning $70k per month.

By writing in this way, you show the recruiter exactly what you have done and what value you offer to the new company.

17. WRITE FOR THE COMPUTER – THE USE OF KEYWORDS

It is very common these days for employment agencies, recruitment consultants, and employers to enter résumés directly into searchable databases. This means that résumés are scanned using OCR (Optical Character Recognition) software. Once in the database, the recruiters can search for particular skill sets by **keywords** and **key phrases**.

What does this actually mean when writing your résumé? Quite simply a keyword is a **word, a term,** or a **phrase**, which identifies a skill or attribute that a job position requires.

The Problem

If you don't have the right keywords in your résumé then you might be completely ignored by the software - even though you might be the perfect candidate for the job (but had failed to slip in the appropriate keywords into your résumé). The use of the right keywords is VERY IMPORTANT.

The Solution

When you write your résumé, simply make sure that you are using the correct words / terms / phrases that describe the job that you are applying for. This is actually very easy and will tend to happen naturally.

For example - let's consider relevant keywords for a 'Pharmaceutical Sales Manager' position.

If your 'Pharmaceutical' sales résumé contains words and phrases such as 'pharmaceutical sales,' 'drug industry' and 'sales manager' then this would – via the OCR scanning software - convey to a recruiter that you probably had sales experience within the pharmaceutical industry.

Try to ensure that you sprinkle your résumé liberally with a variety of appropriate keywords. If you feel that your résumé does not capture the breadth of keywords that apply, then you can have a separate **Keywords** heading on your résumé, where you will summarise them.

And now... that the basics have been covered, let's build your résumé...

IN SUMMARY

Here are the highlights of what has been discussed

1. Keep your résumé short – no more than 2 pages

2. Make it brief, accurate, easy to read and pleasant to the eye...

3. Put the most important information on page 1...

4. Don't be modest about stating your achievements

5. Write in first person

6. Use verbs and action words

7. Remove article words as much as possible...

8. Give numbers and specific examples of accomplishments

9. Use numbers properly

10. Keep an upbeat positive tone

11. State good points and leave off bad points...

12. Borrow credibility from successful companies if you worked for them

13. Tell the truth

14. Take extra care to make sure the résumé has no spelling errors

15. Only put on the résumé what is required for the job and not information that could be troublesome – like race and age

16. Follow the Problem-Action-Result principle

17. Liberally sprinkle keywords throughout the résumé

3

ENTRY LEVEL & NON-EXECUTIVE PERSONNEL

WRITE YOUR RÉSUMÉ – ENTRY LEVEL & NON-EXECUTIVE

At this point in the book, we split the reader requirements into two chapters. This chapter is dedicated to those people who are looking for an entry level or non-executive sales position.

Chapter 4 is dedicated to those people who need a résumé for a more experienced type of job application.

If you in the right chapter, let's get started.

You now know the essential, basic principles required to write your sales résumé. Now let's look at the résumé itself – the format to adopt and the information to include.

In the appendix section, there is a full résumé template complete with a brief description of what is included under the headlines above.

Most sales résumés, especially entry level and those applying for non-executive positions, will take on the following form...

1. RÉSUMÉ HEADER

The résumé header is the most important part of your résumé as it is your contact details: your **name**, **address**, **telephone number(s)** and **email**. The résumé header resides at the top of the résumé.

Your name should be on line 1, whilst the other details (address, telephone number(s) and email) should sit on line 2, and (if necessary) line 3. The name can be aligned to the left or to the centre.

RÉSUMÉ HEADER

RÉSUMÉ HEADLINE / PERSONAL STATEMENT

SUMMARY OF QUALIFICATIONS

PROFESSIONAL EXPERIENCE

QUALIFICATIONS AND TRAINING

AWARDS

AFFILIATIONS

KEYWORDS

Your name should be in **bold** and should be at the top of **both pages** of your résumé. Make your name one font size larger than the rest of your résumé.

It's important to include an email address - a private email - not a work email. If you don't have one then visit **gmail.com**, **hotmail.com** or **yahoo. com** and sign up for one, it only takes 10 minutes. Gmail email addresses are the most respected of the three for its implied stability and permanence. Make sure you have a plain businesslike email address and not something that is more appropriate kept between friends.

For the telephone information, use your private (home) telephone number and / or your mobile telephone number. Don't have a prospective employer calling you at your work.

Try and fit the address / telephone numbers (include a mobile if you can) / email on a single line if possible. Make sure that you separate natural chunks of information with bullet points (*). If they don't fit across a single line then use two lines instead. The résumé header should look like this:

Paul Watson

23 Custer Road * Boston, MA * 0123 456 789 (home),
0712 345 678 (mobile)* Paul_Watson@gmail.com

Paul Watson

23 Custer Road * Boston, MA * 0123 456 789 (home),
0712 345 678 (mobile)* Paul_Watson@gmail.com

Or if you prefer you can align your name to the left hand margin like this...

Paul Watson

23 Custer Road * Boston, MA * 0123 456 789 (home),
0712 345 678 (mobile)* Paul_Watson@gmail.com

Paul Watson

23 Custer Road * Boston, MA * 0123 456 789 (home),
0712 345 678 (mobile)* Paul_Watson@gmail.com

---

2. RÉSUMÉ HEADLINE / PERSONAL STATEMENT

This section follows your name and contact details, so it needs to grab the reviewers' attention

It should display your main selling points and must persuade an employer to read the rest of your résumé. Include the following points to make the most of your skills:.

- Write your résumé headline / personal statement using powerful introductory descriptive text such as - **accomplished, effective, talented, proactive, and successful.**

- Include your field of expertise such as - **Pharmaceutical Sales Representative, Sales Manager, Account Manager, and Business Development Expert.**

- It's a good idea to make your level of experience clear at the beginning - **Manager, Executive,** and **Assistant.** If you wish to be vague on this point, then just describe yourself as a **Professional.**

- If you are already working in the actual Industry then make sure to convey that fact as well.

Make your résumé headline / personal statement in **bold**, in *italics* and centre aligned. Try to keep the headline down to 1 or 2 lines. In order to encourage the employer to keep reading - **do not finish the headline with a period / full stop**

Here are some sales résumé headline / personal statement examples:

Pharmaceutical Sales Representative who consistently over-achieves Target, seeking a Sales Manager position

Award winning Senior Account Manager with excellent sales, marketing and presentation skills within the Business Stationary Industry

Extremely successful Medical Sales Manager, a team player with 7 years industry experience

Enthusiastic and highly motivated sales professional who is expert in developing and maintaining relationships with the medical profession

Successful and ambitious Sales Representative with 5 years experience seeks Telecoms Sales Manager position

Award winning Sales Representative with a record in growing business year-on-year seeks position as Medical Sales Representative

---

Experienced, goal orientated medical professional with program management & client relations experience. Intending to obtain a Pharmaceutical Sales position

Talented sales professional with five years business to business sales, seeking a pharmaceutical sales position

Award winning Sales Representative with a record in growing business year-on-year seeks position as Media Sales Consultant

Next comes your summary of qualifications, which support and flesh out your headline by way a summary of your best assets that you bring to the table...

3. SUMMARY OF QUALIFICATIONS

You may also call this section **Key Skills** (instead of **Summary of Qualifications**) if you wish.

Your résumé headline / personal statement should have already indicated what can do for the employer. Your summary of qualifications now develops your credibility. This section includes:

- A summary of your key skills,

- Your best experience

- Your top achievements acquired throughout your career

- Your academic training

- Your personal life - if it is relevant to the job

What to Include in Your SUMMARY OF QUALIFICATIONS

The emphasis here is **skills, achievements,** and **contribution.**

Make sure you convey **industry specific expertise details** including **years of experience**, any **awards** that you have won and **job relevant training & qualifications**. This can be a good place to state a higher degree if you feel it's appropriate (you'll also state it in the **Qualification & Training** section lower down).

Make sure to:

- Quantify the sales that you have achieved, including the degree and number of time that you have achieved / over achieved target

- Detail the products sold

- List your new business / business development successes

- State relationship management activities that have maintained healthy accounts and / or caused others to flourish

- Add any training or coaching that you have given to other staff

This is also a good place to present your **soft skills** such as:

- Being an excellent communicator

- Trained to be a great coach

- Adept at multi-tasking

- Expert at giving presentations

- Excellent team-working skills

How to Present Your Key Skills

You should present these key skills as **bullet points** - you need approximately **five to seven** bullet points. Make them sharp and to the point.

And once again - this is not a place for modesty. You must really, REALLY sing your own praises. Don't hold back, let the employer have both barrels – tell them why you are so darn good!

Look at this set of Key Skills for a Telecoms Equipment Account Manager:

SUMMARY OF QUALIFICATIONS:

- Skilled Account Manager with history of creating year-on-year growth of up to 250%.

- Accomplished Business Development expert working with clients in Telecoms and Internet Services.

- Developed & clinched a series of $Million winning bids worth in excess of $15M over the last 3 years.

- Project Managed from 'Order to Supply' a series of bespoke Network Switches to a key customer.

- Awarded 'Sales Person of the Year' in 2008.

- Excellent Communication skills at all levels.

You will notice that each of the points above demonstrates a **skill**, an **achievement** or a **contribution**. Let's quickly examine each of the points listed above.

- Skilled Account Manager with history of creating year-on-year growth of up to 250%.

  ◊ **Skill – Sales Growth. Contribution**

- Accomplished Business Development expert working with clients in Telecoms and Internet Services.

  ◊ **Skill – Business Development**

- Developed & clinched a series of $Million winning bids worth in excess of $15M over the last 3 years.

  ◊ **Skill - Bid Management. Achievement**

- Project Managed from 'Order to Supply' a series of bespoke Network Switches to a key customer.

  ◊ **Skill – Project Management. Achievement**

- Awarded 'Sales Person of the Year' in 2008.

  ◊ **Achievement**

- Excellent Communication skills at all levels.

  ◊ **Skill – Communication**

With your key skills presented, you now need to set them within the context of your professional work experience.

4. PROFESSIONAL EXPERIENCE

Starting with your current job and working backwards through your career history, you will present a cohesive and comprehensive summary of your professional experience to supports your job application.

- **Start** with the most significant and tangible information first (that gives the **biggest impact**) and then, move down your list of professional experience credentials. For your present job, you'll need 4 – 7 such bullet points.

- The further that you go back in time, the less relevant your experience (usually) becomes.

- Anything beyond 10 years back, you should just mention the company's name, your position and the time period that you were there and only if the experience is pertinent to the current application.

- If you have only worked for one employer for the last 25 years, simply list the different jobs that you have held over during this time. It will still demonstrate job progression over the years.

- Don't leave any gaps in your career experience if you can help it. After all, you *were* doing something – on sabbatical learning Mandarin? Travelling the world? Doing voluntary work? Studying? Maternity leave?

- You can hide 6 months lounging on the beach in Thailand easily by presenting Job 1 between 2005 – 2007 and Job 2 between 2007 – 2009 (you were on the beach between May – October 2007).

- In particular, – and so far as possible - you need to demonstrate your **achievements** by way of **experience**.

- Remember to apply **Problem-Action-Result** (PAR) rules from chapter 2. If a course of action was a solution to a problem, then try to convey what the **problem** was, the **action** you took, and the subsequent **result**.

- It is likely that you are applying for work, which is similar to and / or builds upon your current work experience - so it is stands to reason that you should give greater space on your résumé to your current job.

- You must specify your **responsibilities** (i.e. the elements of your job – the job description) and your **accomplishments** (sales generated, people recruited, targets beaten, staff developed, customers acquired etc) along the way.

- Don't forget to **quantify** – **how many** years / **how much** profit / **how many** accounts / **how many** people did you manage / **how many** units did you sell.

- Identify **additional training** that you may have received if it is relevant.

- And if you have demonstrated **innovation and imagination** that was clearly beneficial to the company in some other way then you should mention these as well. For instance, your initiatives may have: **driven more business / saved costs / facilitated a better sales process / solved problems**.

How to Present Your Professional Experience

- Write in **concise sentences** and review chapter 2 - Résumé Writing Basics

- When you write about your **present job**, you should use the **present tense**

- When you write about your **previous jobs**, you should use the **past tense**

Here is an example of Professional Experience that conveys the person's success as an Account Manager working in the Telecommunications sector.

PROFESSIONAL EXPERIENCE

Engineering Supplies Inc., Santé Fe NM

Account Manager .... **December 2005 - Present**

- Grew sales of Gateway switches by 150+% each year for the last 3 years

- Opened up business with new 5 new clients in Middle East in 2007.

- Streamlined and enhanced process for delivery of higher value bespoke solutions, reducing lead-time by 3 months.

- After increasing business by 200% in last fiscal year, was awarded Top Sales Person for 2008.

- Liaise with numerous in-house departments to facilitate timely handover of time critical business.

Sales Support Engineer .... **2004 – 2005**

- Worked in pre-sales to ensure that optimum engineering solution was provided to customer before contract was concluded and work commenced.

- In post-contract stage liaised with new clients through to final design, installation, & handover of solution.

- Prepared detailed 'starter pack' for client at handover.

- Engaged in-house client support services via web-based / email based / 24 hour phone support mechanisms. Provided full client data sheet including detailed specification, SLA, points of contact and their escalation process.

- Worked on 6+ new accounts at a time, requiring strong planning & multi-tasking skills.

Installation Engineer ....**1999 – 2003**

- Worked as part of small team installing switch and gateway facilities.
- Hard working & committed, often worked 12-hour days / day and weekends to complete installation on time.
- Travelled over USA / Canada & International to Europe.
- Commenced studies (distant learning) in 'Advanced IP Switching Protocols.'

Keystone Supplies & Installation, Chicago, IL

CAD Design Engineer ....**1997 - 1999**

- Created assembly drawings for the construction and housing of communication multiplex equipment.
- Worked from initial site survey reports. Required CAD interpretation, then the mapping of Keystone equipment into site provided.
- Worked closely with Site Survey Engineer' and 'Provisioning Department' to provide best & most economical solution.
- Designed duct layout, DDF positioning, primary, & reserve power feeds and fire emergency equipment.
- Upon completion, the design was verified by Senior Engineer, prior to handover to installation team for implementation.

5. QUALIFICATIONS & TRAINING

In this section, you should include both formal qualifications (high school / university) and any relevant training courses that you have attended throughout your career.

Give more focus to the education that is most relevant and to the higher level of education.

Common sense is required here. If you have a MBA then the fact that you (obviously) have a high school diploma is somewhat less relevant to your résumé. If you are out of high school since ten years, then don't mention the high school at all. Follow these rules when stating your qualifications:

- **PhD** – Subject, Location, Year
- **Masters Degree / Bachelors Degree** – Major Subjects, Location, Year

- **Masters Degree** - Major Subjects, Location, Year
- **Bachelors Degree** - Major Subjects, Location, Year

- **Bachelors Degree** - Major Subjects, Location, Year

- **High School Diploma**

If you don't have a high school diploma or any formal training then don't include a **Qualifications & Training** section in your résumé.

On the other hand, if you have training but no high school diploma then simply change the heading and include just a **Training** section to your résumé.

If you studied at university but did not complete it for some reason, or even if you failed your degree, you should still list the university and the major subjects studied as:

Studied (Major Subjects), at (Location), during (Years).

List your training also:

Subject 1, Location, Year

Subject 2, Location, Year

List your qualifications and then your training, always placing the most recent at the top.

6. AWARDS

If you have received awards, particularly in your professional career, then you need to highlight them within the context of **Summary of Qualifications and Professional Experience.**

Awards demonstrate **achievements** – and all employers are looking for achievers! If you are several years past high school, then don't mention any awards from this time.

You should also create this separate heading **Awards** after your **Qualifications & Training** section to re-empathise them.

7. PROFESSIONAL AFFILIATIONS

Any professional affiliations that you have can be beneficial in supporting your job application. At the very least, they demonstrate a longevity in and commitment to your industry. Likewise, memberships present a dedication to a community of interest.

Always, list the affiliations in order of relevance.

8. KEYWORDS

A keyword is a **word**, a **term**, or a **phrase** that identifies a skill or attribute that is required for a job. Keywords are 'looked for' by the special OCR software, which scans your résumé. If certain keywords are found during this scan then your résumé will be associated with a particular job that correlates to those keywords.

You will have naturally sprinkled your résumé with good keywords. However, it won't hurt to have a separate **Keyword** section in your résumé to list synonyms, syntax, and terminology that would support your application.

Example Keywords (Telecoms Equipment Sales):

KEYWORDS

Account executive, sales executive, account manager, NexTone, Cisco

IS THERE ANY OTHER INFORMATION TO INCLUDE IN THE RÉSUMÉ?

For the vast majority of sales positions, the résumé that you have just created will now contain all of the information required from you at this stage. Other information that you *may* wish to present under separate headings are as follows (list *before* the **Keywords** section):

If you have foreign language skills, list under a heading called **Languages**.

If you edit or write for an associated published or online publication then list under a **Publications** heading.

For any other skill or data that you wish to convey then simply add a heading which allows you to list the additional information. The bottom line is – if you have a skill or a piece of experience that supports your intended career then you can include it on your résumé.

Congratulations! The end is in sight.

You have now created your sales résumé. However, before you use it to apply for a particular position, please read chapter 5 - to learn how to customize the résumé.

Feel free to skip chapter 4 as this chapter is dedicated to those needing to create a résumé for experienced or executive personnel.

See you on chapter 5.

IN SUMMARY

This chapter is all about the résumé for the Entry Level and Non-Executive Personnel sales people. The important sections are as follows:

1. Résumé Header – this is your name and contact information

2. Résumé Headline or Personal Statement – this is the attention grabbing statement of one or two lines that says who you are and what you are looking for.

3. Summary of Qualifications and Key Skills – where you list your 'skills,' 'achievements,' and 'contribution.'

4. Professional Experience – Listing the most recent or most important job position first then work backwards, presenting a comprehensive summary of your professional experience

5. Qualifications and training – here you list your training and education – giving your focus to the training that has the most relevance.

6. Awards – list any applicable awards with the most recent first

7. Affiliations – list in the order of most relevant

8. Keywords -include this section if your job position has many synonyms

9. Languages – include this section if you can read and/or write different languages

10. Publications – another section to include if you edit or write for an associated published or online publication

4

EXPERIENCED PERSONNEL & EXECUTIVES

WRITE YOUR RÉSUMÉ – EXPERIENCED PERSONNEL & EXECUTIVES

If you are reading this chapter, it is probably because you have a great deal of experience in your field and you need to write a résumé that accommodates and highlights your skill set.

From chapter 3, you know the basic writing skills required for résumé writing and the style that is required. Now let's look at the résumé itself – the format to adopt and the information to include in your sales résumé.

This will be your sales résumé format:

RÉSUMÉ HEADER

EXECUTIVE PROFILE

PROFESSIONAL EXPERIENCE

PROFESSIONAL AFFILIATIONS

AWARDS

AFFILIATIONS

KEYWORDS

In the appendix section, there is a full résumé template complete with a brief description of what is included under the headlines above.

1. RÉSUMÉ HEADER

The résumé header is the most important part of your résumé as it is your contact details: your **name**, **address**, **telephone number(s)** and **email**. The résumé header resides at the top of the résumé.

Your name should be on line 1, whilst the other details (address, telephone number(s) and email) should sit on line 2, and (if necessary) line 3. Align it to the left or the centre.

Your name should be in **bold** and should be at the top of **both pages** of your résumé. Make your name one font size larger than the rest of your résumé.

It's important to include an email address - a private email - not a work email. If you don't have one then visit **gmail.com**, **hotmail.com** or **yahoo.com** and sign up for one, it only takes 10 minutes. Gmail email addresses are the most respected of the three for its implied stability and permanence. Make sure you have a plain businesslike email address and not something that is more appropriate kept between friends.

For the telephone information, use your private (home) telephone number and / or your mobile telephone number. I doubt you want a prospective employer calling you on your work telephone.

Try and fit the address / telephone numbers (include a mobile if you can) / email on a single line if possible. Make sure that you separate natural chunks of information with bullet points (*). If they don't fit across a single line then use two lines instead.

The résumé header should look like this:

Paul Watson

23 Custer Road * Boston, MA * 0123 456 789 (home),
0712 345 678 (mobile)* Paul_Watson@gmail.com

Paul Watson

23 Custer Road * Boston, MA * 0123 456 789 (home),
0712 345 678 (mobile)* Paul_Watson@gmail.com

Or if you prefer you can align your name to the left hand margin like this...

Paul Watson

23 Custer Road * Boston, MA * 0123 456 789 (home),
0712 345 678 (mobile)* Paul_Watson@gmail.com

Paul Watson

23 Custer Road * Boston, MA * 0123 456 789 (home),
0712 345 678 (mobile)* Paul_Watson@gmail.com

---

2. EXECUTIVE PROFILE / SUMMARY

For highly experienced personnel and for those people applying for executive positions, the résumé combines résumé headline / personal statement and summary of qualifications, normal sections in an entry level or non-executive résumé, into a single paragraph of about 10 lines called an **Executive Profile (**or **Summary** if you prefer).

You are an expert in your field (which involves sales of course) with many years experience under your belt and / or you are applying for a sales management position. Either way, your résumé is expected to convey several years of suitable work experience and achievements. It is likely that you will have industry / academic affiliations, awards as well as other Industry specific credentials.

You are going to capture the most important elements of these in your executive profile and then the rest of your résumé will flesh it out in more detail.

You may recall in chapter 2 - Résumé Writing Basics, I wrote about **borrowing credibility** – which is where you leverage off the good name / success / credibility of a company you do / have worked for (e.g. a Fortune 1000) company. If you have that, then your profile is an excellent place to mention it – it will enhance **your credibility**!

Your profile is not an essay. It needs to be one paragraph of approximately 10 lines showing comprehensive, eye-grabbing text. At the very least, this section needs to capture the following points:

- Years of experience

- Areas of expertise

- Most impressive achievements

- Top / most relevant soft skills

Profile

Results driven Sales Manager with over 10 years experience delivering above quota results, managing & developing successful account teams within the Business Stationary market. Strategic thinker and market analyst with track record in creating winning sales & marketing strategies that consistently over deliver against target. Excellent presentation and communication skills have led to a series of innovative & successful multi-$million alliances with international clients across Europe & Middle East. Expert team builder, coaching sales teams to greater success year after year.

Example of Profile (Senior Sales – Business Stationary):

3. PROFESSIONAL EXPERIENCE

This is your career history section. Starting with your current job and working backwards, you will present a cohesive and comprehensive summary of your professional experience to support your job application.

- **Start** with the most significant and tangible information first (that gives the **biggest impact**) and then, move down your list of professional credentials. For your present job, you will need approximately 10 bullet points.

- The further back in time, then the fewer bullet points you'll be required to give, since the further you go into your history, the less relevant your experience (usually) becomes.

- If you have only worked for one employer for the last 25 years, simply list the different jobs that you held within the company. It will still demonstrate job progression over the years.

- Don't leave any gaps in your career experience if you can help it. After all you **were** doing something – on sabbatical learning Mandarin? Travelling the world? Doing voluntary work? Studying? Maternity leave?

- If the above point is a problem for you, then this is a useful tip for you...you can hide 6 months lounging on the beach in Thailand easily by presenting Job 1 between 2005 – 2007 and Job 2 between 2007 – 2009 (you were on the beach between May –

October 2007!).

- In particular, – in so far as possible - you need to demonstrate your **achievements** by way of **experience**.

- As you specify your **responsibilities,** (i.e. the elements of your job – the job description) and your **accomplishments such as:**

  ◊ Sales generated

  ◊ People recruited

  ◊ Targets beaten

  ◊ Staff developed

  ◊ Customers acquired

- Be sure to emphasize those elements (skills) most often associated with a **high achiever** in your sales field. These may include:

  ◊ Organizational skills

  ◊ Strategic capability

  ◊ Management & motivation of staff

- Don't forget to **quantify – how many** years / **how much** profit / **how many** accounts / **how many** people you managed / **how many** units you sold / how much money you saved.

- If you have demonstrated **innovation and imagination** clearly beneficial to the company in some other way - then you should mention these. For instance, your initiatives may have: **driven more business / saved costs / facilitated a better sales process / solved problems**. You may have achieved this by:

  ◊ Alliances and joint ventures

  ◊ Outsourcing

  ◊ Introducing new processes

Add anything that demonstrates RESULTS, RESULTS, and RESULTS!

Here are some powerful phrases that you, as an executive, may wish to include:

- Problem-solving

- Decision-making

- Performance and productivity improvement

- Oral and written communications

- Team-building

- Leadership

- Customer retention, and

- Strategic planning

How to Present Your Professional Experience

- Write in **concise sentences**- review chapter 2 - Résumé Writing Basics

- When you write about your **present job**, you should use the **present tense**.

- When you write about your **previous jobs**, you should use the **past tense**.

Anything beyond 20 years back, you should just mention the company's name, your position and the years that you were there.

Professional Experience example (Senior Sales – Business Stationary):

On the next page…

PROFESSIONAL EXPERIENCE

TRESCO CORPORATION, Boston, MA............................**2004 - present**

National Sales Manager

- Manage team of 12 Major Account Managers selling into large corporate clients across USA & Canada. Includes establishing new accounts & developing present accounts. Work with team to ensure targets are met. Authorized to respond to RFPs and other proposals. Work with White Label partners to address smaller corporate market.

- Grew team sales to $18 million from $13M in 3 years. Anticipated sales for current fiscal year are $20M.

- Migrated key customers to higher margin products increasing margin by 23%.

- Won new $5M customer in 2008 from major competitor.

- Responded to and closed 10+ deals on RFP basis for key accounts - 60% gross margin and $7 million in annual sales.

- Led project team to design & implement new order-to-delivery system. New process reducing order-to-delivery time - and so invoice & collection - by 30%.

- Established effective competitive sales strategy, which increased North American sales presence and hence profits.

- Instigated partner program that has led to 50% increase in sales of Presentation Systems.

- Initiated annual product seminar for major clients. Working with an external Events Company, hold 2-day seminars for top clients. Events serve to highlight new products for next financial year, enhancements to current product suite and – importantly - to solicit feedback from clients about their strategic needs in the short, medium, and long term.

CAPTION COMPANY Boston, MA ....**1999 - 2004**

Senior Account Manager

- Designed and launched Sales Website, which established a global presence overnight and grew international sales from zero to $3M in 1st 12 months.

- Re-focused sales team on high margin products - downsized existing sales team and then recruited up-skilled team members. Led training for new staff to hone necessary knowledge base.

- Increased sales by $3.2 million by identifying and introducing products to meet consumers' needs that changed as a result of market conditions.

- Established contact with new 3rd party agents to address untapped market at low cost. Led contract negotiations, designed compensation plan and signed up 7 new partners on a franchise basis. Grew sales to sector by 350% in 18 months.

- Held weekly 1-hour sales meetings; monthly ½-day meetings – inc. guest speakers, training & monthly awards and every 6 months - off-site informal gatherings for account development feedback and strategic planning.

TIMES ADMIN CORP, Boston MA ....**1997 - 1999**

Account Manager & Account Executive

- Focused on Small Business Accounts. Re-focused efforts, closed 30% accounts and grew margin by 35% in 9 months.

4. AFFILIATIONS

As a long-term professional in your particular field of expertise, it is probable that you'll be affiliated with one or more industry groups. If you are, then you need to display this on your résumé under a new heading. Being affiliated demonstrates an interest and a commitment to your industry. This is something that can readily separate you from other equally qualified applicants.

You need to list - in order of relevance - the body with whom you are affiliated. If you hold a position within that body, then state what it is and give a brief description of that role as well as any significant achievements.

Other Memberships:

Also, include any charitable or community associations that you have a membership to. You need to state the entity with which you are linked, your position and give a brief summary of your role and achievements.

5. AWARDS

As a professional of some experience and standing, you may have received various awards and accolades over the years. Even if you have already mentioned them previously in your résumé (for instance in your **Profile/Summary**) put them again in this section. As with the previous heading, 'Affiliations' this section is vitally important since it can readily distinguish you from other equally qualified candidates.

6. EDUCATION

If you have a college degree(s), possibly a post graduate qualification, diplomas as well as other relevant industry qualifications then list them in order starting with your most recent at the top, then work backwards in time.

For each item, state the college, location and the major subjects studied. It is not necessary to give the year attained (especially since it could have been 10 – 20 years ago).

*Note - if there is greater relevance by shifting the order, then change the order accordingly – with most important & relevant in first place.

7. KEY WORDS

A keyword is a **word**, a **term,** or a **phrase** that identifies a skill or an attribute that is required for a job. Keywords are 'looked for' by the special OCR software, which scans your résumé. If certain keywords are found during this scan then your résumé will be associated with a particular job that correlates to those keywords.

You will have naturally sprinkled your résumé with good keywords. However, it won't hurt to have a separate **Keyword** section in your résumé to list synonyms, syntax, and terminology that would support your application.

Example Keywords (VP Sales, Business Stationary):

> **KEYWORDS**
>
> Sales manager, senior manager, director, VP, Assistant VP

IS THERE ANY OTHER INFORMATION TO INCLUDE IN THE RÉSUMÉ?

For the vast majority of sales positions, the résumé that you have just created will now contain all of the information required. Other information that you *may* wish to present under separate headings are as follows (list *before* the **Keywords** section):

If you have foreign language skills, list under a heading called **Languages**.

If you edit or write for an associated published or online publication then list under a **Publications** heading.

For any other skill or data that you wish to convey then simply add a heading which allows you to list the additional information. The bottom line is – if you have a skill or a piece of experience that supports your intended career then you can include it on your résumé.

Congratulations! The End Is In Sight

You have now created your sales résumé. However, before you use it to apply for a particular position, please read chapter 5 - to learn how to customize the résumé.

See you on chapter 5.

IN SUMMARY

This chapter was written for the Experienced & Executive Level Positions.

1. Résumé Header – this is your name and contact information

2. Executive Profile – this is the 10 line attention grabbing text showing your experience and achievements industry / academic affiliations, awards as well as other Industry specific credentials.

3. Professional Experience – Start with your current job and work backwards through your career to show a comprehensive summary of your professional experience, which supports your job application.

4. Professional Affiliations – this is your list of professional associations – always listed in order or relevance.'

5. Awards – list any applicable awards with the most relevant first

6. Education – list degrees, diplomas and other industry qualifications in order with the most recent first

7. Keywords -include this section if your job position has many synonyms

8. Languages – include this section if you can read and/or write different languages

9. Publications – another section to include if you edit or write for an associated published or online publication

5

CUSTOMIZE

YOUR RÉSUMÉ

CUSTOMIZE YOUR RÉSUMÉ FOR THE JOB

'Because if you aim at nothing, you'll hit it every time!'

You should have now prepared your résumé according to the methods set out in chapters 1 – 4, depending upon your experience and level of the position that you are applying for.

Chances are you have written your sales résumé with a particular position in mind or you'll have prepared it as a generic résumé that can then be targeted for specific jobs.

If the former, then it's ready to send out on a speculative basis – i.e. registering your résumé with recruitment agencies, posting to employment bulletin boards / websites etc.

Whichever approach you had in mind as you prepared your résumé, the résumé will need some fine-tuning before you can use it to apply for a particular job posting. That is what we're going to look at now.

BACKGROUND INFORMATION THAT YOU'LL NEED

By knowing exactly what the job posting requests, you can tweak your résumé to fit the precise requirements of the job posting. You are going to make it easy for the reviewer to spot you as an ideal candidate.

You should have a clear idea of the job requirements from the job ad, whether from a newspaper, an online website, recruitment agency, or even from the company itself. Ideally, you will have a **detailed job description**.

At the very least, you should know:

- The job title

- A description of the role

- What experience is required

- What qualifications are expected

WHERE DOES THE INFORMATION COME FROM?

If you are lucky, you have something like a descriptive newspaper ad that has all of the desired information already. If you don't have something like this, then you need to find out the required information in other ways.

This could involve calling up the company and speaking to the hiring manager (the person you'll work for is **much better** than HR). If it's convenient, you might even take them out for a coffee. You will need to make it clear that you are **not asking** for the job – you are simply asking for **more information** about the position before you decide to apply or not.

Or if a recruitment agency has been engaged to sort through the applicants or to carry out the first round of interviews, then speak to them – they will have the details you need.

It's also a good idea to do some background research on the company through the internet to get a better idea of their products and services.

Once you have the information you need, you can fit your résumé to fit the requirements of the job ad.

Let's look at how you do this...

HOW TO CUSTOMIZE YOUR RÉSUMÉ FOR A SPECIFIC JOB AD

First, you need to review the job description and your sales résumé.

Then extract from your résumé, the most relevant (and impressive) experience, and qualifications (the 'credentials') and include them in your résumé headline / summary of qualifications for non-executive résumés or in your profile for executive résumés.

Making these changes is an immediate green flag, highlighting you as a good potential candidate.

The next steps are to:

- Go through your résumé and where possible present your experience in a way that it matches - as much as possible - the experience that they are looking for.

- Work through this process paying careful attention to the language that they have used in the job description then attempt to use the same language, the same terminology in your résumé. This includes key words that they have used (like specialized, expert in, driven, etc) and use them in your résumé.

- Don't be afraid to remove material from your résumé - if it's clearly irrelevant to what's mentioned in the job ad – that way you keep your résumé tight & focused. Don't remove anything that relates to powerful soft skills or impressive achievements.

If you take the time to refine your résumé as above, you will demonstrate that you are applying for *this job* and NOT just *any job* and that you have the credentials that they are looking for.

Following on the theme of customizing your résumé, it's important to follow the same steps for your résumé cover letter. A good cover letter is the icing on the cake. Let's look at writing a great, but simple résumé cover letter that's going to get your sales résumé read...

IN SUMMARY

Targeting your résumé means tweaking the same résumé slightly to fit the job you are applying for

1. Check the job description, looking for the specific skills and qualities they are looking for

2. Extract from your résumé the most relevant pieces of your experience and qualifications and make sure they are included in your résumé headline / summary of qualifications for non-executive résumés or in your profile for executive résumés.

3. Go through your résumé and where possible present your experience in a way that it matches - as much as possible - the experience that the job position states they are looking for.

4. Pay attention to the specific language used in the ad and try to use the same language that they have used

5. Remove any irrelevant material to keep the résumé tight and focused for that position you are applying for. Don't remove anything that relates to powerful soft skills or impressive achievements.

6

RÉSUMÉ COVER LETTERS

ICING ON THE CAKE – A GREAT COVER LETTER

When applying for a specific job, your résumé will go to the reviewing / recruiting person. This person may work for the company or may be an intermediate 3rd party such as a recruitment consultant. Either way, your résumé will usually need to be accompanied by a cover letter.

Don't neglect your résumé cover letter. It is the first contact between you and the recruiting body. A simple well-constructed cover letter will ensure that your résumé is reviewed for the position that you are applying for.

The vital ingredients of a résumé cover letter are:

- Salutation to the recruiting person – if that means calling the company to find out who will be looking at your résumé – then do it

- Reference to the position that you are applying for – recruiting companies hire for many positions – don't make them search what job you are applying for, because they won't, they will throw yours out first

- How you found out about the position – state the ad / newspaper / website etc

- Include the name of the mutual contact if you have one

- Use a *brief* summary of your best qualities to match the requirements of the position

- Present your contact details for follow up

- Be brief, to the point and less than a page in length

THINGS TO DO WHEN YOU WRITE YOUR COVER LETTER

Writing your cover letter isn't a hard job, and it is just as important as your résumé. Therefore, follow a few of these easy guidelines to make sure your cover letter gets the response it deserves:

- Use a standard business letter format

- Focus the letter on what you can offer the company

- Do not copy another person's cover letter

- Use a conversation style of writing

- Spell check, proofread and then check again

- Remember to sign the cover letter

THING NOT TO DO WHEN WRITING YOUR COVER LETTER

Just as it's important to follow certain guidelines, it helps to know what to avoid doing when writing important letters like these.

- Avoid using stiff or awkward writing

- Don't be **creative** or **unorthodox**

- Be sure your tone doesn't across as arrogant or superior

- Don't use acronyms that may not be easily understood – recruiters are not necessarily aware of the details of your industry

- Make the mistake of using Internet chat language or slang in the letter

- Never inflate your capabilities

If you follow these rules, the cover letter should give you the opening you need for the interview.

Example Résumé Cover Letter for this position:

Position – Media Sales Consultant – Outside Sale

Source – Michigan Daily Post, September 25th 2008

Reference MDP/MSC

Responsibilities:

- Generating and Maintaining New Accounts

- Reviewing, Managing, and Growing Existing Account Base

- Meeting Publication and Online Deadlines

- Achieving Sales Quotas/Goals

Qualifications:

- Bachelors Degree Preferred

- Basic Computer Skills and Working Knowledge of the Internet

- Two Years of Successful Outside Sales Experience Preferred

- Strong Presentation and Effective Communication Skills

- Professional Attitude

- Reliable Transportation, Valid Driver's License and Proof of Insurance

Résumé Cover Letter:

Name
Title
Company
Address
City, State, Zip Code

Paul Watson
23 Custer Road
Boston
MA 34211
0123 456 789 (home)
0712 345 678 (cell phone)
Email Paul_Watson@hotmail.com

27th September 2008

Dear Sir (or Mr. Smith if you have the name),

Please find attached my résumé in application for the Media Sales Consultant position (Reference MDP/MSC), which appeared in the Michigan Daily Post on September 25th 2008.

In particular, please note that I am a graduate and an award winning Sales Executive.

My experience includes:

- Generating, maintaining and growing New Accounts
- Reviewing, Managing, and Growing Existing Account Base
- Meeting Deadlines

I look forward to hearing from you at your earliest convenience. If you require any additional information then please do not hesitate to get in touch.

Yours sincerely,

Paul Watson
0123 456 789 (home)
0712 345 678 (cell phone)
Email Paul_Watson@gmail.com

This cover letter is brief, to the point and conveys that you have the experience the company is looking for according to their ad. Note how the same terminology has been used **back to them** in the letter as was **used by them** in the job description.

The cover letter is in harmony with your résumé, which will demonstrate that your experience fits (or at lends itself to) the requirements of the position.

IN SUMMARY

Cover letters are just as important as your résumé. They are the first thing that a recruiter or hiring manager will look at.If he or she doesn't like it, chances are your résumé won't even be opened.

To make the best cover letter:

- Have the correct salutation to the recruiting person

- Reference the position that you are applying for

- State how you found out about the position

- Include the name of the mutual contact if you have one

- Use a 'brief' summary of your best qualities to match the requirements of the position

- Present your contact details for follow up

- Be brief, to the point, and less than a page in length.

- Use a standard business letter format

- Focus the letter on what you can offer the company

- Do not copy another person's cover letter

- Use a conversation style of writing

- Spell check, proofread and then check again

- Remember to sign the cover letter

- Avoid using stiff or awkward writing

- Don't be 'creative' or 'unorthodox'

- Be sure your tone doesn't across as arrogant or superior

7

AFTERWARDS

SO YOU HAVE AN EXCELLENT COVER LETTER AND RÉSUMÉ – NOW WHAT...

There are a couple of simple steps that need to be underlined here.

If you are mailing or dropping off your résumé and cover letter in person -

1. Make sure you use a good quality paper and that the ink in the printer is relatively new for a crisp clean print job.

2. Resist the urge to use colored paper or bright graphics to jazz up your documents.

3. Use a business envelope with a typed address if possible. You may think your handwriting is neat but not everyone will.

4. If mailing, remember to use adequate postage.

5. If dropping the résumé off in person, remember your appearance and demeanor. The receptionist who you see may not be the same person who interviews you but don't ever overestimate the power she has over your application. If you are rude to her, that bit of information will make its way to the hiring manager and you won't ever be considered.

If you are emailing your résumé, do you know what form this electronic transfer needs to be in? If the job description doesn't specify, save the documents in rtf or PDF format, so that the formatting stays like it should. Don't have any fancy formatting in your résumé as the formatting does not end up the same as when you emailed the document.

If you are posting the résumé to a website, like Monster.com or Workopolis. com then follow the posted instructions to make sure your résumé shows the most professional look it can.

After you have sent of your résumé and cover letter - what do you do?

Now, because you know that you've done everything that needs to be done, this is a great time to brush up on your interviewing skills.

Why?

With that great résumé, full of keywords and targeted to one specific job the next step has to be...

– an interview!

8

APPENDIX

KEY ACTION WORDS

Be sure to pepper your résumé with action words in order to qualify and enhance your skills, ability, and successes. The following may help...

Accomplished	Collected	Disproved	Formulated
Achieved	Communicated	Dissected	Founded
Achievement	Compared	Distributed	Gathered
Acted	Compiled	Diverted	Gave
Activated	Completed	Drafted	Generated
Adapted	Composed	Dramatized	Guided
Addressed	Computed	Drew	Handled
Adjusted	Conceived	Drove	Headed
Administered	Conceptualized	Edited	Helped
Advised	Conducted	Educated	Hypothesized
Aided	Conserved	Effected	Identified
Allocated	Consolidated	Eliminated	Illustrated
Altered	Constructed	Empathized	Imagined
Analyzed	Contracted	Enabled	Implemented
Anticipated	Controlled	Encouraged	Improved
Applied	Coordinated	Enforced	Improvised
Appraised	Corrected	Engineered	Incorporated
Approved	Corresponded	Enhanced	Increased
Arbitrated	Counseled	Enlisted	Influenced
Arranged	Created	Established	Informed
Ascertained	Critiqued	Estimated	Initiated
Assembled	Dealt	Evaluated	Initiative
Assessed	Decided	Examined	Innovated
Assigned	Defined	Executed	Inspected
Assisted	Delegated	Expanded	Inspired
Attained	Delivered	Expedited	Installed
Audited	Demonstrated	Experimented	Instituted

Authored	Described	Explained	Instructed
Balanced	Designed	Expressed	Integrated
Brought	Detailed	Extracted	Interpreted
Budgeted	Detected	Fabricated	Interviewed
Built	Determined	Facilitated	Introduced
Calculated	Developed	Familiarized	Invented
Catalogued	Devised	Fashioned	Inventoried
Chaired	Diagnosed	Filed	Investigated
Charted	Directed	Financed	Judged
Checked	Discovered	Fixed	Kept
Clarified	Dispatched	Followed	Launched
Classified	Dispensed	Forecast	Learned
Coached	Displayed	Formed	Lectured
Led	Predicted	Reorganized	Studied
Lifted	Prepared	Repaired	Succeeded
Listed	Prescribed	Reported	Summarized
Listened	Presented	Represented	Supervised
Loaded	Printed	Researched	Supplied
Logged	Prioritized	Reshaped	Supported
Made	Problem Solving	Resolved	Surpassed
Maintained	Processed	Responded	Surveyed
Managed	Produced	Restored	Symbolized
Manipulated	Programmed	Retrieved	Synergized
Marketed	Projected	Reunited	Synthesized
Mediated	Promoted	Reviewed	Systematized
Memorized	Proofread	Revised	Tackled
Modeled	Protected	Rewrote	Talked
Moderated	Provided	Risked	Taught
Modified	Publicized	Scheduled	Tended
Molded	Published	Screened	Tested
Monitored	Purchased	Searched	Trained
Motivated	Questioned	Secured	Transcribed
Navigated	Raised	Selected	Translated
Negotiated	Read	Separated	Traveled

Observed	Realized	Served	Treated
Obtained	Reasoned	Set goals	Troubleshot
Offered	Received	Set Up	Tutored
Operated	Recommended	Sewed	Typed
Ordered	Reconciled	Shaped	Unified
Organized	Recorded	Shared	United
Originated	Recruited	Showed	Updated
Outlined	Redesigned	Simplified	Upgraded
Overhauled	Reduced	Sketched	Upheld
Oversaw	Reevaluated	Sold	Used
Painted	Referred	Solved	Utilized
Perceived	Refined	Sorted	Verbalized
Performed	Rehabilitated	Specified	Warned
Persuaded	Rejected	Spoke	Washed
Photographed	Related	Started	Weighed
Piloted	Remodeled	Stimulated	Wired
Planned	Rendered	Streamlined	Worked
Played	Renegotiated	Strengthened	Wrote

RÉSUMÉ TEMPLATES

Entry Level & Non-Executive Personnel

AND

Experienced Personnel & Executive

ENTRY LEVEL & NON-EXECUTIVE PERSONNEL

This section provides a template for the résumé format typically used for people entering sales and for those applying for non-executive positions.

Assuming that you have read chapter 2, you should be aware of the writing style for writing your résumé. This means that you will be writing with brevity, clarity and conveying on-target useful data to an employer.

Chapter 3 then fully describes the format and the content that your résumé should follow.

Chapter 5 showed you how to tweak your résumé to match a specific job to correlate your skills and education to the specific requirements of the position.

YOUR NAME

Address * City, State * Telephone (home), Telephone (mobile) *
Your_Email@YourEmailProvider.com

Your headline conveys your top selling points, area of expertise & level of experience. Use powerful introductory descriptive text & include your most powerful and useful skills. 2 or 3 lines max; don't finish with a period

SUMMARY OF QUALIFICATIONS:

- Here you aim to capture your key skills, your most useful experience, and top achievements.

- This is no place for modesty – really sing your own praises.

- Include those skills that you have acquired throughout your career, from academic training, and even in your personal life if they support your case.

- Aim to have 5 to 7 such bulleted points.

- Be sure to quantify sales and demonstrate growth.

- You can also include any soft skills here.

- If you won awards then mention them.

PROFESSIONAL EXPERIENCE

THIS IS THE NAME OF YOUR CURRENT EMPLOYER

Present Job Title..Year 1 - Present

- Using the writing tactics described in Chapter 2, you are going to give a concise summary of your relevant career experience.

- Starting with your current job and working backwards through your career history, present a comprehensive summary of your professional experience

- Demonstrate your **achievements** by way of **experience**!

- Most likely, you are applying for work, which is similar to and / or builds upon your current work experience - so give greater résumé space to your current job than your previous jobs.

- Focus on responsibilities and your accomplishments. Don't forget to quantify – how many sales / how much growth / how many people etc.

- Aim for 4 – 7 points for your current job.

Previous Employer

Previous Job Title...Year 2 – Year 1

- As described above. Aim for 4 or 5 quality points.

Previous Employer

Previous Job Title...Year 3 – Year 2

- The further back in time you go, then (usually) the less relevant it is to your next career move, so aim for fewer points of about 3 or 4 quality points.

Previous Employer

Previous Job Title...Year 4 – Year 3

- Anything that is from over 10 years ago, just mention the company name, your position and the length of time you served.

QUALIFICATIONS AND TRAINING

List in order of study or of relevance to your education

You should include both formal qualifications (high school / university) and any relevant training courses that you have attended throughout your career.

Give more focus to the education that is most relevant.

AWARDS

If you have received awards, particularly in your professional career, then you must highlight them within the context of 'Summary of Qualifications' and 'Professional Experience.' Awards demonstrate 'achievements' – and all employers are looking for achievers!

You should also create an 'Awards' heading after your 'Qualifications & Training' section to re-empathize them.

AFFILIATIONS

Any professional affiliations can be very beneficial as they demonstrate a longevity in and commitment to your industry. Likewise, memberships present a dedication to a community of interest - list in order of relevance.

KEYWORDS

You will quite naturally have sprinkled your résumé with good keywords already. However, it does no harm to have a separate section in your résumé called 'Keywords,' especially if various synonyms exist for your job keywords.

EXPERIENCED PERSONNEL & EXECUTIVES

This section provides a template for the résumé format typically used for experienced sales personnel and for those applying for executive positions.

Assuming that you have read chapter 2, you should be aware of the writing style for writing your résumé. This means that you will be writing with brevity, clarity and conveying on-target useful data to an employer.

Chapter 4 then fully describes the format and the content that your résumé should follow.

Chapter 5 showed you how to tweak your résumé to match a specific job to correlate your skills and education to the specific requirements of the position.

YOUR NAME

Address * City, State * Telephone (home), Telephone (mobile) * Your_Email@YourE-mailProvider.com

EXECUTIVE PROFILE

You are an experienced individual and you may be climbing the executive ladder by applying for an Executive post. Your Profile is not an essay – it is one paragraph consisting of approximately 10 lines of comprehensive, eye-grabbing text. Your Profile needs to capture the following points:

How many years of experience you have / your areas of expertise / most impressive achievements / your top most relevant soft skills

PROFESSIONAL EXPERIENCE

THIS IS THE NAME OF YOUR CURRENT EMPLOYER

Present Job Title .... Year 1 - Present

- Starting with your current job and working backwards through your career history, present a comprehensive summary of your professional experience

- Demonstrate your **achievements** by way of **experience**!

- Most likely, you are applying for work, which is similar to and / or builds upon your current work experience - so give greater résumé space to your current job than your previous jobs.

- Focus on responsibilities and your accomplishments. Don't forget to quantify – how many sales / how much growth etc.

- Be sure to adopt a brevity and sharpness to your writing as described in Chapter 2.

- Aim for about 10 points for your current job.

THIS IS THE NAME OF YOUR CURRENT EMPLOYER

Previous Job Title 1.. Year 2 – Year 1

- As described above. Aim for 4 or 5 quality points.

THIS IS THE NAME OF YOUR CURRENT EMPLOYER

Previous Job Title 2.. Year 3 – Year 2

- The further back in time you go, then (usually) the less relevant it is to your next career move, so aim for fewer points of about 3 or 4 quality points.

THIS IS THE NAME OF YOUR CURRENT EMPLOYER

Previous Job Title 1...**Year 4 – Year 3**

For any positions from 10 years ago, just mention the company name, your position, and the length of time you served.

AFFILIATIONS

It is likely that you'll be affiliated with one or more industry groups, which demonstrates an interest and a commitment to your industry. This is something that can readily separate you from other candidates.

List all affiliations in order of relevance. If you hold a position within that body, then state what it is and give a brief description of that role as well as any significant achievements.

Other Memberships:

It is perfectly acceptable to include any charitable or community associations that you have memberships with. You need to state the entity with which you are linked, your position and a brief summary of your role and achievements.

AWARDS

As a professional of some experience and standing, you may have received various awards and accolades. Even if you have already mentioned them previously (for instance in your 'Profile') put them under this heading. As with the previous heading, 'Affiliations,' this section is vitally important since it can readily distinguish you from other equally qualified candidates.

EDUCATION

It's quite likely that you have a college degree, a post graduate qualification, diplomas, as well as other relevant industry qualifications. List the certifications starting with your most recent, and then work backwards in time.

For each item, state the college, location and the major subjects studied. It is not necessary to give the year attained (especially since it could have been 10 – 20 years ago!).

KEYWORDS

You will have naturally sprinkled your résumé with good keywords already. However, it does no harm to have a separate Keyword section in your résumé especially if various synonyms exist for your job keywords.

RÉSUMÉ TEMPLATES

Entry Level & Non-Executive Personnel

AND

Experienced Personnel & Executive

ENTRY LEVEL & NON-EXECUTIVE PERSONNEL

The sample résumé on the next page is an example of a sales résumé, which would be used by new entrants and those in sales at a non-executive level.

Notice the writing style that has been used as per chapters 2 and 3. These techniques make the sales résumé succinct, clear and convey on-target useful information.

When you are applying for a specific job, your résumé will need to be tweaked, as described in chapter 5, to correlate to the job in question.

PAUL HOPKINS

23 Custer Road * Boston, MA * 0123 456 789 (home),
0712 345 678 (mobile) * Paul_Hopkins@gmail.com

Award winning Account Manager with Commercial & Technical Expertise. Has over 10 years experience in the Telecommunications Equipment Market

SUMMARY OF QUALIFICATIONS:

- Highly skilled & successful Account Manager.
- Accomplished Business Development expert working with clients in Telecoms and Internet Services.
- Developed & clinched a series of $Million winning bids worth in excess of $15M over the last 3 years.
- Project Managed from 'Order to Supply' a series of bespoke Network Switches to a key customer.
- Awarded 'Sales Person of the Year' in 2013.
- Excellent Communication skills at all levels.

PROFESSIONAL EXPERIENCE

Engineering Supplies Inc, Santé Fe NM

Account Manager, ...December 2005 - Present
- Grew sales of Gateway switches by 150+% each year for the last 3 years
- Opened up business with new 5 new clients in Middle East in 2007.
- Streamlined and enhanced process for delivery of higher value bespoke solutions, reducing lead-time by 3 months.
- After increasing business by 200% in last fiscal year, was awarded Top Sales Person for 2008.
- Liaise with numerous in-house departments to facilitate timely handover of time critical business.

Sales Support Engineer .... 2004 – 2005

- Worked in pre-sales to ensure that optimum engineering solution was provided to customer before contract was concluded and work commenced.
- In post-contract stage liaised with new clients through to final design, installation, & handover of solution.
- Prepared detailed 'starter pack' for client at handover.
- Engaged in-house client support services via web-based / email based / 24 hour phone support mechanisms. Provided full client data sheet including detailed specification, SLA, points of contact and their escalation process.
- Worked on 6+ new accounts at a time, requiring strong planning & multi-tasking skills.

Installation Engineer .... **1999 – 2003**

- Worked as part of small team installing switch and gateway facilities.
- Hard working & committed, often worked 12-hour days / day and weekends to complete installation on time.
- Travelled over USA / Canada & International to Europe.
- Commenced studies (distant learning) in 'Advanced IP Switching Protocols.'

Keystone Supplies & Installation, Chicago, IL

CAD Design Engineer .... **1997 - 1999**

- Created assembly drawings for the construction and housing of communication multiplex equipment.
- Worked from initial site survey reports. Required CAD interpretation, then the mapping of Keystone equipment into site provided.
- Worked closely with Site Survey Engineer,' and 'Provisioning Department,' to provide best & most economical solution.
- Designed duct layout, DDF positioning, primary, & reserve power feeds and fire emergency equipment.

Upon completion, the design was verified by Senior Engineer, prior to handover to installation team for implementation

RT Laundromat Franchise, Maintenance Engineer..........................**1996 - 1997**

Whilst studying at college had part time job (weekends) maintaining & servicing washing machines in Laundromats across Chicago.

QUALIFICATIONS AND TRAINING

- Enhanced Sales Using NLP
- Advanced IP Switching Protocols – Diploma 9 Months
- University of Illinois-Chicago, Chicago, IL
- BSc Applied Engineering

AWARDS

2008 Sales Person of the Year.

AFFILIATIONS

Telecom Engineering Association US

KEYWORDS

Account executive, sales executive, accounts manager.

EXPERIENCED PERSONNEL & EXECUTIVES

The sample résumé on the next page is an example of a sales résumé, which would be used by new entrants and those in sales at a non-executive level.

Notice the writing style that has been used as per chapters 2 and 4. These techniques make the sales résumé succinct, clear and convey on-target useful information.

When you are applying for a specific job, your résumé will need to be tweaked, as described in chapter 5, to correlate to the job in question.

FRANK HOPKINS

25 Custer Road * Boston, MA * 0123 456 987 (home), 0712 345 876 (mobile) Frank_ Hopkins@gmail.com

PROFILE

Results driven Sales Manager with over 10 yrs experience of delivering above quota results and managing & developing successful accounts teams within the Business Stationary market. Strategic thinker and market analyst with track record in creating winning sales & marketing strategies that consistently over deliver against target. Excellent presentation and communication skills, which has led to a series of innovative & successful multi-$million alliances with international clients across Europe & Middle East. Expert team builder and coaching sales teams to greater success year on year.

PROFESSIONAL EXPERIENCE

TRESCO CORPORATION, Boston, MA 2004 - present

National Sales Manager

- Manage team of 12 Major Account Managers selling into large corporate clients across USA & Canada. Includes establishing new accounts & developing present accounts. Work with team to ensure targets are met. Authorized to respond to RFPs and other proposals. Work with White Label partners to address smaller corporate market.

- Grew team sales to $18 million from $13M in 3 years. Anticipated sales for current fiscal year is $20M.

- Migrated key customers to higher margin products increasing margin by 23%.

- Won new $5M customer in 2008 from major competitor.

- Responded to and closed 10+ deals on RFP basis for key accounts - 60% gross margin and $7 million in annual sales.

- Led project team to design & implement new order-to-delivery system. New process reducing order-to-delivery time - and so invoice & collection - by 30%.

- Established effective competitive sales strategy, which increased North American sales presence and hence profits.

- Instigated partner program, which has led to 50% increase in sales of Presentation Systems.

- Initiated annual product seminar for major clients. Working with an external Events Company, held 2-day seminars for top clients. Events serve to highlight new products for next financial year, enhancements to current product suite and – importantly - to solicit feedback from clients about their strategic needs in the short, medium, and long term.

CAPTION COMPANY Boston, MA   1999 - 2004

Senior Account Manager

- Designed and launched Sales Website, which established a global presence overnight and grew international sales from zero to $3M in 1st 12 months.

- Re-focused sales team on high margin products - downsized existing sales team and then recruited up-skilled team members. Led training for new staff to hone necessary knowledge base.

- Increased sales by $3.2 million by identifying and introducing products to meet consumers' needs, which changed as a result of market conditions.

- Established contact with new 3rd party agents to address untapped market at low cost. Led contract negotiations, designed compensation plan and signed up 7 new partners on a franchise basis. Grew sales to sector by 350% in 18 months.

- Held weekly 1-hour sales meetings; monthly ½-day meetings – inc. guest speakers, training & monthly awards and every 6 months - off-site informal gatherings for account development feedback and strategic planning.

TIMES ADMIN CORP, Boston MA   1997 - 1999

Account Manager & Account Executive

- Focused on Small Business Accounts. Re-focused efforts, closed 30% accounts and grew margin by 35% in 9 months.

AWARDS

Sales Person of Year, Caption Company, 2000 and 2002

Top Account Manager, Times Admin Corp, 1998

AFFILIATIONS

Member, Trade Association of Stationary Manufacturers

Associate Member, American Society of Association Executives

EDUCATION

Advanced Sales, In Assoc with American Sales Guild

University of Michigan, MBA, Business & Marketing Studies

KEYWORDS

Sales manager, senior manager, director, VP, Assistant VP

ADDITIONAL RESOURCES

JOB WEBSITES

The sites listed have a good selection of sales jobs.

www.salesjobs.com

www.sellingcrossing.com

www.salesheads.com

www.salescareersonline.com

www.theladders.com

www.salestrax.com

www.monster.com

www.hotjobs.com

www.indeed.com (Generic job search engine, good for sales)

You'll see a current summary of these and other websites here:

http://www.writeasalesresume.com/resources/

INDUSTRY SPECIFIC RESOURCES

Pharmaceutical & Healthcare Sales

www.medreps.com

www.zenopa.com

www.starmedical.co.uk

IT Sales

www.itsalesprofessionals.com

You'll see a current summary of these and other websites here:

http://www.writeasalesresume.com/resources/

INTERVIEWS

If you can answer these questions then you should be ok:

blog.sironaconsulting.com

You'll see a current summary of interview help and other websites here:

http://www.writeasalesresume.com/resources/

I should hope that after reading this book you won't need either of these products; but just in case you're feeling idle...

RÉSUMÉ WRITING SERVICES

If having read this book you feel that you don't have the time or the inclination then you could always outsource the task to a 3rd party. If you do, then make sure that you check their work first - ask to see examples of their work, and be sure that they use the methodology and techniques that I describe in the book.

Two website where you'll have huge amounts of résumé writers to choose from are Guru.com and Elance.com. Both have freelancers and companies who register their skills and services that they outsource to people like you and me. You just need to create a 'free' account then post your project (to write your sales résumé) under the appropriate section.

Also, since all of the freelancers and companies listed will have provided their personal profile and portfolio of projects (e.g. résumés), you can peruse them at your leisure, find and then list them and then invite them to take up your particular résumé project.

It may sound a bit complicated but it's a cinch. Just takes a few minutes to register and then 10 minutes to post your project.

Remember - before you award your résumé writing task to anyone, do make sure to look at their résumé examples. If they are no good then don't use them. In summary look for quality - someone who uses the techniques that I have described in my book. Do not award your résumé to someone based on cost alone!

Here they are again:

Guru.com

Elance.com

Also if you do a search on your favorite search engine you will find hundreds of companies offering their services. The same guidelines apply as using Guru and Elance.

Current summary of résumé outsourcing can be found here:

http://www.writeasalesresume.com/resources/

RÉSUMÉ WRITING SOFTWARE

There are a few out there. The one that I have come across a few times that's been recommended to me (I am not endorsing it, just repeating what I've heard) is called 'Amazing Resume Creator'. Naturally it is not specific to sales, but there is no reason why you can't overlay our magic as you go

Note that it will set you back just under 40 bucks, but it's easy to use and takes a lot of the hard work out of the résumé writing. Simply download to your computer and away you go. Check it out here:

Amazing Resume Creator

Current résumé writing software that's worth considering may be found here:

http://www.writeasalesresume.com/resources/

****

*If you use any of the services or software listed above then please let me have any feedback on how they performed – positive or negative - so that I can consider for future editions. Likewise, if you have any other service or product suggestions then do let me know please.

CONTACT

For all comments and feedback including ideas for making this book even better, please contact me via my email: Chris@iCareerPro.com.

Visit the website: www.WriteASalesResume.com